Are Those Animals
REAL?

Are Those Animals REAL?

How Museums Prepare Wildlife Exhibits

Judy Cutchins and Ginny Johnston

Foreword by Ralph J.T. Bauer

WILLIAM MORROW AND COMPANY
New York 1984

PHOTO CREDITS
Permission for the following photographs is gratefully acknowledged: Courtesy of the Library Services Department, American Museum of Natural History, pp. xvii (photo: Judy A. Cutchins), 11 (neg. no. 123879), 31 (photo: Judy A. Cutchins), 55 (photo: Judy A. Cutchins), 56 (neg. no. 324761, photo: Rota), 57 (photo: Judy A. Cutchins); Bob Connell, p. 52; Judy A. Cutchins, pp. xiv-xvi, xix, 2-3, 5, 7-9, 13-14, 20-29, 32-34, 36-51, 53, 58-62, 64-70; Fernbank Science Center, pp. xiii, 15, 63; Charles Fleming, p. 35 both; Steven C. Hartman, p. xviii; G. A. Septon, Milwaukee Public Museum, pp. 16-19; Joel Volpi, p. 1.

Printed in the United States of America.

10 9 8 7 6 5 4 3 2 1

Book design by Kathleen Westray

Library of Congress Cataloging in Publication Data

Cutchins, Judy.   Are those animals real?
Includes index. Summary: An introduction to the methods and materials museum artists use to prepare animals for display in dioramas and exhibits.
1. Taxidermy—Juvenile literature. 2. Zoological models—Juvenile literature. 3. Zoological specimens—Collection and preservation—Juvenile literature. 4. Museum techniques—Juvenile literature. [1. Taxidermy. 2. Museum techniques. 3. Zoological models] I. Johnston, Ginny. I. Title. QL63.C88 1984   069.5′3   84-1049
ISBN 0-688-03879-4
ISBN 0-688-03880-8 (lib. bdg.)

Acknowledgments

The authors wish to express sincerest thanks to the following people for their encouragement and technical assistance during the writing of this book:

The exhibit staff of the American Museum of Natural History, New York City;

Ralph Bauer, manager of exhibits, American Museum of Natural History;

Bob Connell, wildlife artist and taxidermist, Fernbank Science Center, Atlanta, Georgia;

Charles Fleming, curator and taxidermist, Georgia State Capitol Museum, Atlanta, Georgia;

Mozelle Funderburk, molding and casting specialist, Fernbank Science Center;

Steven C. Hartman, science director, Museum of Arts and Sciences, Macon, Georgia;

Joseph Hurt, taxidermist and diorama specialist, Joseph Hurt Studio, Atlanta, Georgia;

Richard L. Morrison, exhibit designer, Fernbank Science Center;

Greg Septon, taxidermist, Milwaukee Public Museum;

Ed Thompson, taxidermist and museum curator, Fernbank Science Center.

To all the young museum visitors
whose question—"Are those animals *real?*"—
inspired the writing of this book

Contents

Foreword

This book offers a wealth of information for all those children who have visited a natural history museum and asked, "Are those animals real?" Now the authors reveal one facet of museum exhibition with considerable expertise, explaining the technical details of those lifelike exhibits. This revelation will not, however, detract from what our late president, Gardner D. Stout, enjoyed saying was "pure magic" when describing the exhibits to our visitors at the American Museum of Natural History.

Twenty children viewing an exhibit at a museum will take away twenty different experiences, for each of us sees with a distinctive sharpness refined by our parents, teachers, training, and our own past experiences. This book should open many more eyes.

For those of us concerned with this field of artistic endeavor—museum exhibition—there is the hope that this book will stimulate the enthusiasm of some to consider a career in museum work. Those who follow that path will carry on for future generations, creating for them what may very well be the most direct contact with wildlife they will ever experience.

Ralph J.T. Bauer
MANAGER, EXHIBITION
American Museum of Natural History
New York, 1984

Wildlife Exhibits

How can an animal look so real but not be alive?
That's a good question and one a lot of people ask
when they see wildlife exhibits in museums. Most of
the animals in the exhibits were alive at one time. After
they died, their skins were preserved to last for many
years. Museum artists worked to make the animals
look alive again.

Ducks are carefully placed in a pond exhibit.

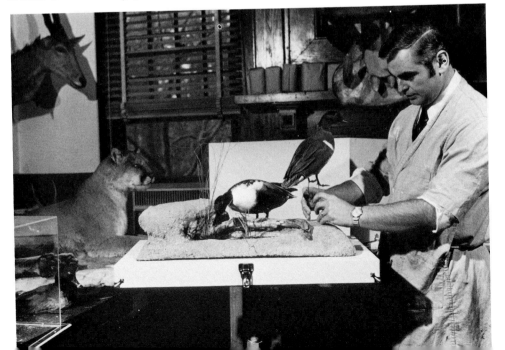

Other animals in exhibits were never alive. They are lifelike models of real animals. To create them, the artists first have to study the real animals carefully to learn how each one looks and moves.

This lifelike box turtle is actually a rubber model.

A jungle habitat is the perfect setting for this Colybus monkey.

Once prepared for the museum, the animals and models are exhibited for visitors to see and enjoy. Some are displayed in dioramas. These exhibits show how wild animals really live in nature.

An African diorama at the Anniston Natural History Museum in Alabama.

Some dioramas are of woodland scenes. Others are of jungles or deserts or grasslands. Dioramas can even show what life is like underwater!

Atlantic white-sided dolphins leap playfully in this underwater diorama.

Museum visitors get to see the skeleton of a prehistoric ground sloth.

A giant animal may be an exhibit all by itself, and a very small animal can be shown "larger than life."

Let's visit a science museum and find out some ways animals are displayed for visitors to see.

The garden spider may be two inches in real life but two feet as a larger-than-life model.

This beetle collection shows specimens from all over the world.

1.
Mounting Godzilla Gorilla

How much does a gorilla weigh? The one the museum artists picked up at the zoo weighed almost 800 pounds! Godzilla had been a favorite of zoo visitors for over 20 years before he died. Now, the zoo keepers wanted the artists to make him look alive again.

A real-life gorilla.

They carefully packed the huge animal in ice and stored him in a big freezer until the artists came for him.

To make Godzilla look alive again, the museum artists were going to mount him by putting his skin onto an artificial body.

Mounting Godzilla took many weeks. First, every part of his real body had to be measured so that the artificial body would fit inside the real skin. Then Godzilla's skin with his thick fur coat was carefully removed from the body. The gorilla's soft "insides" were discarded, but the skeleton was saved. Some of Godzilla's bones would be used in making the artificial body form.

An artist carefully measures the gorilla's huge shoulder.

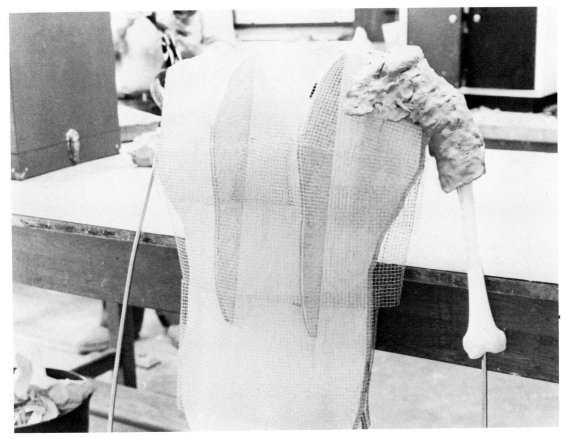

Clay was molded over wire screen to form the gorilla's chest shape.

The gorilla's skin was flown to New York to be tanned. The tanner treated the skin and fur with chemical preservatives that would keep the skin soft and make it last a long time. Even the skin on Godzilla's face was treated.

Meanwhile, at the museum the artists made a wooden body and covered it with wire screen. The screen would create the thick chest shape of the gorilla. Godzilla's real skull was placed on a metal neck rod. His real arm and leg bones were attached to more rods.

The gorilla's powerful muscles were molded in clay.

This framework was covered with clay. The clay was pressed and carefully shaped until it was a sculpture of Godzilla's real body.

Next, the clay body was covered with plaster to make a mold. When the plaster mold was dry and hard, it was cut off the body form. The clay-and-wood body with the real bones was no longer needed.

Godzilla's artificial body was then made by painting layers of paper and glue inside the plaster mold. Metal rods were added to make this papier-mâché body strong. After days of drying, the paper body was removed from the mold. Exact copies of Godzilla's hands and feet were attached.

When the preserved skin came back from the tanner, it was mounted. The skin was stretched and sewn in place on the artificial body. It was a perfect fit! Tanning had caused the gorilla's skin to lose its natural color; so his face, hands, and feet were painted with black wall paint to match his actual dark skin color. The face was polished with a shoeshine brush to make it shine like real skin.

Godzilla's skin begins to look real again.

When the tanned skin was mounted and glass eyes set in place, Godzilla looked alive.

When the museum artists completed the work, Godzilla Gorilla looked exactly as he had in real life, but he weighed less than 100 pounds!

The work that was done on the gorilla at the museum is called taxidermy. It is a very special museum job. The same fur, nose, ears, claws, and whiskers that an animal had when it was alive may be used in mounting it. Only the eyes are different. They are made of glass. On the inside, though, nothing is the same.

Sometimes museum artists buy artificial bodies of mammals and mount the real skins onto them.

These fox and beaver body forms are made of rubber and wire.

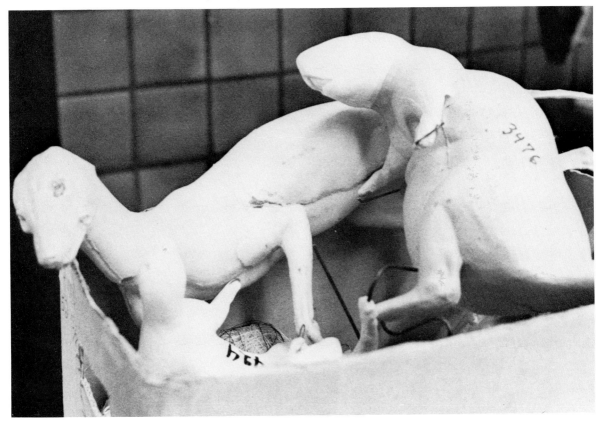

Or artists may carve body shapes out of lightweight foam material or balsa wood. The skins of very small mammals, such as squirrels, chipmunks, and rabbits, can be mounted on straw bodies.

Museum artists may carve small mammal bodies, like the body of this fox squirrel, from foam.

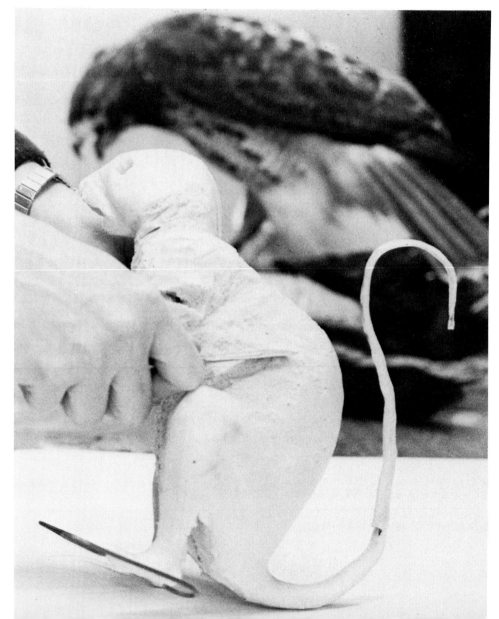

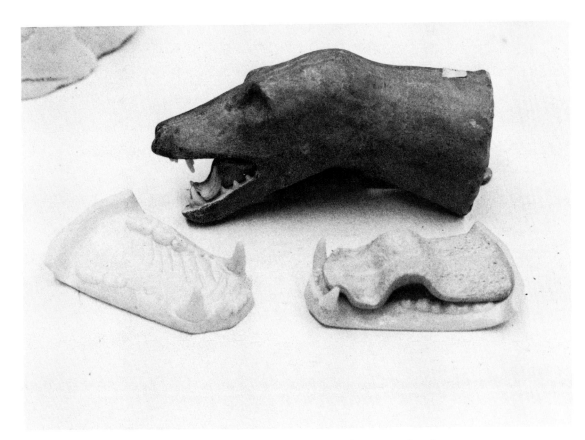

Plastic teeth and tongue are used when mounting an animal
with its mouth open.

Glass eyes, plastic teeth, and papier-mâché heads
help the artists make the animals look real.

Taxidermy is not a new idea. For hundreds of years people have preserved animal skins. Almost 100 years ago, an amazing work of taxidermy was done in the United States on a circus animal. While P. T. Barnum's famous circus was loading animals onto a train, the largest and most popular of all the animals, Jumbo the Elephant, was hit by a train and killed.

Jumbo was so special to people who loved the circus that Mr. Barnum hired a famous taxidermist named Carl Akeley to mount Jumbo. To remove the elephant's skin, Mr. Akeley needed the help of six strong men.

Mounting Jumbo was quite a job, and it took many days. The skin alone weighed 1,538 pounds! Carl Akeley and his helpers stretched the skin onto a huge wooden body. They put in large glass eyes. Jumbo looked alive again! P. T. Barnum had a special train car made for Jumbo so he could still travel from town to town with the circus. Circus lovers had Jumbo back again.

Jumbo amazed circus visitors for many years.

2.
Feathers
Rare and Beautiful

While on a weekend field trip one spring, the museum artists stopped by to see a ranger at a national wildlife refuge. They knew that the ranger had 23 beautiful whistling swans stored in a large freezer. The swans had been found dead on the bank of a lake in the refuge.

Had someone killed all these animals? Well, yes and no. For over 100 years, duck hunters had fired lead shotgun pellets at ducks above the lake. Over the years, millions of the tiny gunshot had fallen into the lake and become matted in the water plants. When the swans ate the plants, they swallowed the lead shot, too. Many of them died of lead poisoning after feeding at the lake for a long time.

The whistling swans were beautiful and the ranger was anxious to see them mounted for a museum to display. The artists returned with three of the birds.

Back at their workshop, the artists began the taxidermy. The animals were skinned. The skins, with feathers still attached, and the real webbed feet were washed and treated with a preservative. An artificial body was made of straw for each bird. This straw body was wrapped with thread until it was the exact size and shape of the real swan. Large wires were used to connect the real skull and leg bones to the straw body. Then the skin was mounted onto it.

Artificial bodies like this can be made for birds of all sizes.

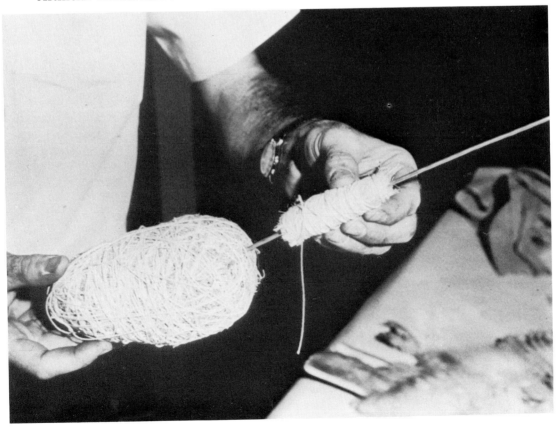

Eye color and size must look exactly like those of the real animal.

New "swan" eyes were chosen from a collection of glass eyes, and they were placed in the head of each bird. The real beaks were touched up with black paint. One swan was mounted with its beak open. An artist made a rubber tongue to put in its mouth.

Black paint was used as a final touch on a real beak.

Nearly invisible wires hang swans from the museum's ceiling.

It took several weeks to finish mounting the whistling swans. When the job was completed, the artists hung the swans from the ceiling of the museum. The birds looked as if they were flying through the air!

Birds on exhibit in museums today may be very old. On the shelves of an old storage room in the Milwaukee Public Museum, an artist found a large jar of alcohol.

It was quite a challenge to make these chicks look alive again.

It contained the wet but preserved bodies of three peregrine falcon chicks. The date on the label showed that the chicks had been in the jar for almost 60 years!

Today peregrine falcons are an endangered species. There are not as many of them now as there once were. The law protects these birds, and no one is allowed to kill them, even for a museum collection. But 60 years ago, peregrines were not a rare or endangered species. Someone at that time had collected them for the museum to mount someday. If the artist could make a lifelike display of them, people who might never see these rare falcons in the wild would be able to enjoy them in a diorama.

The artist searched the museum's storage room for the skin of a mother peregrine falcon to mount with the chicks. Amazingly, he found one, and the label on it read, GOES WITH THREE CHICKS. The artist was excited and ready for a challenging job of taxidermy.

The chick bodies were soaked with alcohol and their feathers were matted from being cramped in the jar for years. The artist had to work very carefully to skin the chicks. After he finished, he rinsed the skins and fixed them with a preservative.

Artificial bodies for the three chicks were made of straw. The mother peregrine's skin was mounted over a body carved of balsa wood. Each skin was stretched onto its artificial body and sewn into place. The chicks' feathers were dried and fluffed with a hair dryer.

A hair dryer becomes a feather dryer for chicks.

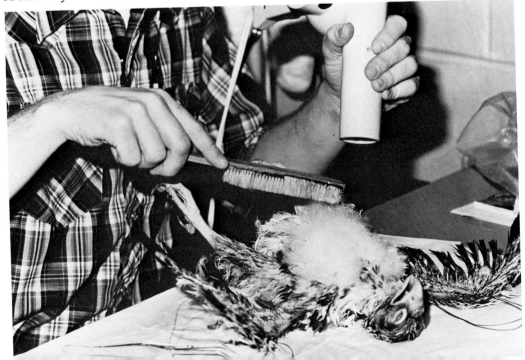

This tongue inside the mother falcon's open beak looks real.

Glass eyes were set in place. Artificial tongues were made and glued inside the mouths. The beaks and tongues were painted with oil paints.

A fluffy chick gets finishing touches.

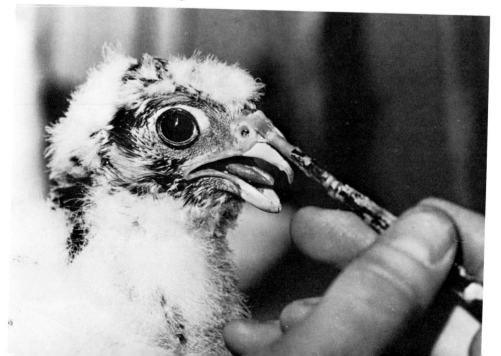

Under the mother's claws, the artist mounted a small bird just as it might have looked if the falcon had killed it to feed her chicks. After weeks of drying, the falcons were ready for display in a rocky ledge nest.

The mounted falcons were placed in a diorama showing their nest, or aerie.

Museums often have exhibits of birds that are rare, endangered, or even extinct.

Because ivory-billed woodpeckers are extinct, they are seen only in museums.

Visitors to the Georgia State Capitol Museum get a chance to see the very rare whooping crane in a natural setting.

3.
Scaly and Slithery Exhibits

One day the herpetologist, or reptile expert, from the nearby zoo brought a box to the museum. One of the zoo's timber rattlesnakes had died, and the zoo officials thought the museum could use it in an exhibit. The museum artist in charge of the reptile displays was pleased. She wanted to make the reptile exhibits bigger and more exciting.

In the museum workshop, the artist placed the snake in the freezer until she decided how she should prepare this beautiful three-and-a-half-foot specimen. There were several things she could do. She could simply put the snake in a jar of alcohol. But a dead snake in a jar is not much of an exhibit—and it certainly isn't lifelike!

She could skin the snake and then stretch its skin over a plaster form. The snake would look real, but because plaster breaks easily, one accident and it would be in a thousand pieces!

Neither of these ideas seemed right for the rattlesnake. The artist decided to make a rubber model that was exactly the same size and shape as the real snake. If it were painted carefully, no visitor would be able to tell the model from the real thing.

Animals preserved in alcohol do not make interesting displays.

Specimens that will be used by the artists are stored in a freezer so they will not decay.

To make the rubber model, or replica, the artist first had to make a plaster mold of the real snake. So she took the timber rattler from the freezer, thawed it out, and gently curved its body into a lifelike position. Then she poured liquid plaster over the top of the snake. This would make a mold of the snake's back and sides. She did not have to make a mold of the bottom half because no one would see it.

When the plaster hardened about an hour later, the snake was carefully removed. The scales had been clearly imprinted in the plaster, and the mold was perfect. The real snake was put back into the freezer. The artist would look at its colors and patterns when she was ready to paint the rubber model.

The clay wall around the snake will hold the plaster in place.

The real rattlesnake is removed from the hardened plaster.

After several days the plaster mold had dried and was ready to be used. The artist poured liquid rubber into the mold. The rubber hardened in about two days, and the artist gently peeled out a rubber rattlesnake. Only the back and sides had been molded, but from the top, the rubber snake looked just like the one in the freezer—except it had no color. Before allowing the

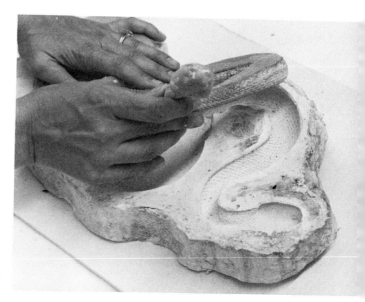

The artist takes the rubber snake from the mold.

The underside of the replica snake will not be seen when the snake is on display so it was not molded.

Patterns of gray and black
mark this timber rattlesnake.

model to dry completely, the artist twisted it into a
coiled position. When it was fully dry, it was ready for
the final step—painting.

Matching the patterns and colors of the real rattlesnake was a very slow and difficult job. But when the
artist was finished, the timber rattler looked ready to
slither away.

The finished rattler blends into this mountain diorama.

When both parts of this mold are put together, they will make a "whole" water snake.

Museums often make plaster molds for replicas of lizards, snakes, small alligators, frogs, toads, and salamanders because these reptiles and amphibians cannot be skinned and mounted as easily as some other kinds of animals. The molds may be in two or more parts so that the whole animal, even its underside, can be displayed. Plaster molds may be labeled, stored, and used over and over again to make models for other exhibits or even other museums.

These rubber reptiles will someday be used in a swamp diorama.

4.
A Great White Shark Arrives

Outside the museum, icicles hung from the bare tree branches. It was a cold, gray winter morning. Inside, the artists walked thoughtfully through the exhibit halls. There were reptiles, birds, insects, and spiders—displays of animals all around—but something was missing . . . something to make the museum more exciting.

As they walked by the shark exhibit, one of the artists said, "I've got it! And I know just where to get what we need."

Soon he was on the phone talking to a friend at another museum 1000 miles away. The friend had just what was needed and said he would send it.

Before long, a heavy crate arrived. The artist carefully opened it and unwrapped several plaster

The shark exhibit makes museum visitors feel they are part of the underwater world.

molds with shapes imprinted in them. From these molds he could make a lifelike great white shark! The most feared of sea creatures, the great white is one of the largest of all the sharks. The molds had been made from a real 17½-foot shark caught in the Pacific Ocean five years before.

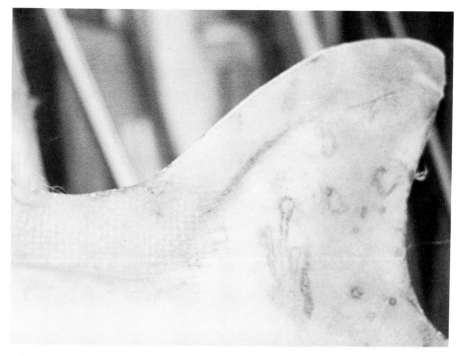

The fin of the real great white was two feet tall.

This giant sea animal would certainly add excitement to any museum exhibit. But preparing it was not going to be an easy task. Since the real great white shark had been so big and long, the plaster molds had to be made in several parts.

The work began. Pieces of fiberglass were pressed into the molds. Then a special liquid that dries hard was painted over the fiberglass in each mold. The combination of fiberglass and this liquid would harden to a very strong yet lightweight material. The molds were then fitted together and the fiberglass material was left to dry and harden. When the molds were taken apart, the new body of the shark was in one big piece, and it was ready for the finishing touches.

Fiberglass fins were made from other molds and attached to the body. Artificial eyes and real shark teeth were glued into place. The artist painted the shark with oil paints to match the real shark's colors. It had taken over 100 hours to make, but the replica looked exactly like a real great white shark.

A fiberglass replica of the giant hammerhead shark will be an exciting addition to the shark exhibit.

Razor-sharp teeth line this huge shark's jaws.

When the shark was placed in the exhibit hall, visitors who saw it were fascinated.

Replicas of smaller fish can be made in the same way. First plaster is poured over the real fish to make a mold. Then an artificial body is made inside the plaster mold. It may be made of fiberglass, rubber, plaster, or even wax.

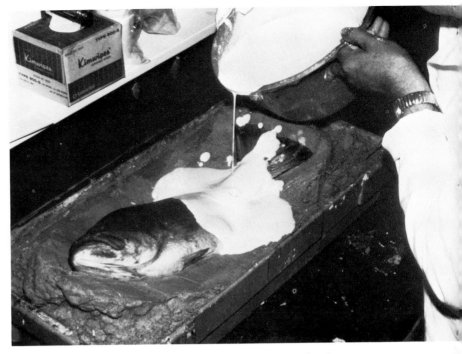

A bass is pressed into wet clay and covered with plaster.

When the plaster dries, the fish is removed and the mold
is ready to be used.

This barracuda gets lifelike teeth, eyes, and a paint job.

Painting the replica is very important. Colors and patterns of the real fish must be carefully matched by the artist. Sometimes the artist even paints the glass eyes so that the color is authentic for the fish.

In most museums, replicas are used instead of real fish because they are sturdier and last much longer.

5.
Preserving Delicate Wings

One fall morning, a beautiful luna moth came into the museum all by itself! During the night, the moth had hidden under the eaves near the front door, but the cold night air killed the delicate insect. When the door was opened the next morning, the moth was blown inside by the breeze.

The unusual luna moth makes a fine museum specimen.

American butterfly collection on display.

The museum artist thought that the moth would be a nice addition to the collection of moths and butterflies, so he decided to preserve it.

The moth had to be taken carefully to the workshop because its wings are delicate. They are covered with tiny scales that are easily rubbed off. Even a gentle touch might damage them. A sharp pin was placed through the abdomen so the insect could be picked up.

The luna moth is spread and pinned.

The artist placed the luna moth on a board. Its large, soft abdomen was given a shot of strong preservative. This chemical would make the moth's body harden and hold its shape. It would also keep it from rotting.

The tiny needle will not damage the moth's body and the preservative injected into it will make the insect last a long time.

The delicate luna moth wings must be very carefully prepared.

The wings were stretched out flat and held in place by tissue paper pinned to the board. The luna moth was left to dry in this position.

By the end of the week, the luna moth that blew in the front door had dried completely. It was ready to be added to the Lepidoptera collection on display.

The soft green and yellow colors in the moth's scales faded as the insect dried out, but the delicate wings were not painted for fear of breaking them. Instead, a color photograph was placed near the real moth to show visitors its true colors.

There are more than 900,000 kinds of insects in the world. If the museum added one new specimen to the collection each day, it would take over 2,000 years to exhibit them all!

This display shows interesting wing patterns.

6.
A Tarantula Gift

Early one summer afternoon a young woman came by the museum with her pet that had recently died. It was a giant western tarantula! The spider was more than six inches across and was in perfect condition. The young lady was sad about losing her pet, and she wanted the museum to preserve it in their spider collection.

The museum artist invited her to come back in about a month when the tarantula would be on display.

This western tarantula died and was brought by its owner to the museum to be preserved.

Small animals, such as the tarantula, are preserved in freeze dryers
of this size.

Once in the workshop, the artist decided to freeze-
dry the spider to preserve it. Freeze-drying requires a
special machine—a freezer that is also a dryer.

Pins are placed across the tarantula's legs to hold them in a realistic position.

To prepare the tarantula for freeze-drying, the artist fixed its body and legs in a lifelike position. A piece of cotton was placed beneath its abdomen to support the body. Each of the spider's eight hairy legs was carefully held in place with crisscrossing pins. The spider was put into the freezer and kept there until it was frozen solid.

Then it was ready for the drying step. The ice in the frozen spider was slowly dried out. Inside the drying chamber, a pump constantly removed the air. Without air, the ice did not melt. Instead, it evaporated directly into water vapor.

It took nearly a week for all the ice to evaporate.

Finally, the spider was a freeze-dried specimen. But it still looked very much alive, with its large, hairy black abdomen and long legs. The tarantula would stay in this perfect condition for a long time if it was handled with care.

Freeze-drying is a method museums often use to preserve spiders, insects, and other soft-bodied animals. Even animals as big as bobcats or foxes can be prepared in very large freeze dryers.

Sometimes museums display small animals, such as spiders, inside clear hard plastic. To do this, the spider's body is injected with a preservative.

The tarantula's abdomen will be plump and round again after the preservative is added.

A variety of small animals is displayed and protected in clear plastic.

Then a layer of clear liquid plastic is poured into a container and allowed to harden. The spider is placed on this layer and more layers of the plastic are added. When the small creature is completely covered and the plastic has hardened, the container is removed.

Visitors can see specimens that are prepared like this from all sides.

7.
Preparing a Giant Praying Mantis

Outside his workshop window, an artist had been watching a fascinating insect—a praying mantis. It lived in a little bush and spent most of the day sitting quietly with its sharply hooked front feet raised and folded.

The folded front feet earned the mantis its nickname: "praying."

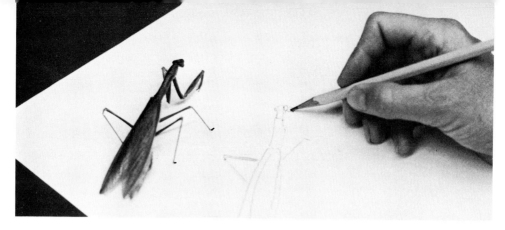

A life-size detailed drawing of the insect is the artist's first job.

The artist thought that the praying mantis would make a wonderful exhibit for the museum. But it would be hard for visitors to see because the real insect was just too small for an exhibit. The praying mantis was only three inches long. The artist wanted to make a giant praying mantis many times larger than life. It would be 25 times larger than the real insect. The model would be six feet long!

Before the artist began to make the model he studied the praying mantis carefully. He took photographs and made sketches from different angles. Then, in the workshop, the hard part of the job began. What could be used to build such a creature? The artist decided to make the head of soft clay. A layer of liquid rubber was painted over the soft clay head. After it dried, the stretchy rubber mold was cut and peeled from the clay head. Liquid plastic was poured into the rubber mold to make the clear plastic head that would be used in the exhibit.

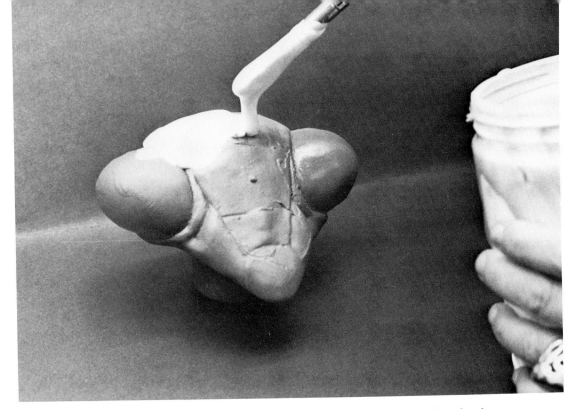

The artist made a rubber mold that would be used to create the plastic mantis head.

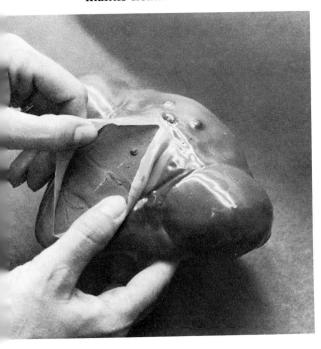

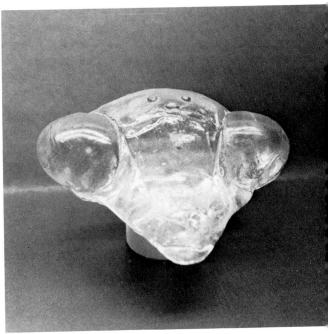

Next, the body and legs were carved from a lightweight foam material. Thin metal rods were pushed into each leg to make the giant mantis strong. The rods also allowed the artist to bend the legs a little for the final shape.

Each spine on the leg is carefully carved in foam.

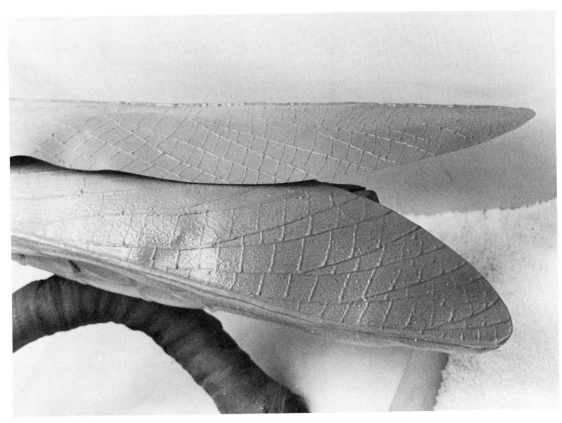

Tile cement was used to make the lines of veins on these giant wings.

The wings were the biggest challenge of all. After cutting the shape from clear plastic sheeting, the artist built up each vein by squeezing tile cement out of a catsup dispenser. This took over four hours.

Finally, the body was put together and coated all over with a special liquid that hardens and dries clear. Then the artist painted the model with oil paints to match the colors of the real praying mantis.

The six-foot praying mantis greets visitors at the museum's front door.

After weeks of work, the giant insect was finished and ready to display.

Museums all over the world exhibit larger-than-life animals—from grasshoppers to spiders to microscopic pond life.

Plants and animals normally seen only under a microscope may be reproduced thousands of times larger for the museum.

8.
Dinosaurs on Display

In one room of the museum there stands an enormous skeleton. The room's ceiling has to be very high because the skeleton is almost 20 feet tall! It is the skeleton of a dinosaur that lived over 100 million years ago.

Remains of ancient teeth and bones are discovered nearly every year in various parts of the world. Why have these things not disappeared over such a long period of time? When dinosaurs and other prehistoric animals died, their bodies decayed. Bones and teeth were the hardest parts of the bodies, so these things decayed more slowly. Some decayed so slowly that the materials in the bones and teeth were gradually replaced by minerals from the soil. This left what looks like bones and teeth, but which are really mineral-rich stones. These "stone bones" are called fossils.

The huge dinosaur skeleton on display was constructed from fossils found many years ago on a museum fossil-collecting expedition. Before being sent to the museum, each fossil bone was cleaned and then painted with shellac to seal and protect it. Then the stone bones were stored carefully in plaster and shipped back to the museum, where the artists built the skeleton.

Museum visitors take a look at duck-billed dinosaurs.

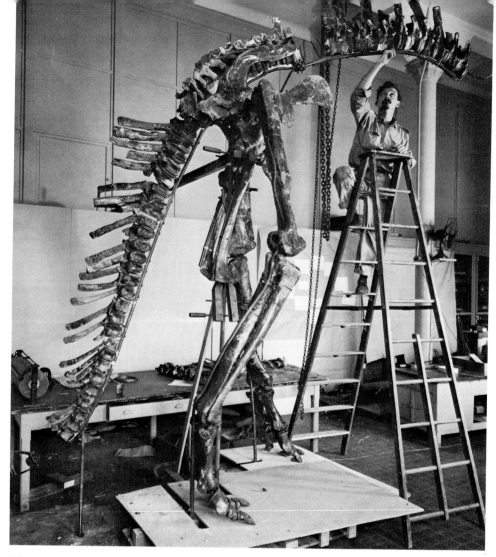

This giant duck-billed dinosaur will be over 30 feet long when its skeleton is completed.

The shape of the dinosaur's body was made with steel rods. Each bone was then attached to this steel frame by wires and screws. The artists and scientists working on the dinosaur used the information they knew about the skeletons of today's animals to help them put the fossil bones together in the right way.

Sometimes fossil bones were missing or too badly damaged to be used. The artist then made fake bones of plaster to replace them. It took over one year to finish assembling the skeleton.

Fossil bones are quite valuable and so are not often used in exhibits. Instead, the museum artists make replicas of them. After the dinosaur skeleton is assembled, the museum artists take it apart and make a rubber mold of each bone. The molds are made by painting liquid rubber onto the bones. After the rubber is dry, the artists use fiberglass to make the molds sturdy. Later the fiberglass and rubber molds are gently peeled off the real fossils. Each stone bone is then safely stored, and the replica bones are made from the molds. Molds can be used over and over to make replica bones.

A replica bone is removed from the fiberglass and rubber mold.

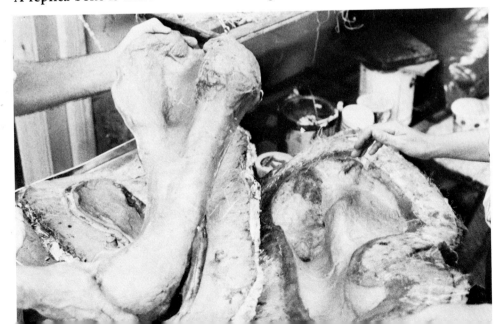

When replica bones are wired together, the dinosaur skeleton looks just like the real thing. Replica skeletons can be shared with museums all over the world.

By studying fossil skeletons and teeth, scientists know the size and shape of prehistoric animals. With this information, artists can imagine how the animals may have moved, what they may have eaten, and other interesting things about how they lived. Models of prehistoric animals can be constructed from a combination of scientific research and an artist's imagination. For example, skin from ancient animals is not often found by fossil hunters. Therefore, artists must guess what prehistoric reptile skin might have looked and felt like when they build a whole dinosaur.

Fossil bones such as these help scientists learn about animals from the past.

Replica skull of *Tyrannosaurus rex* shows six-inch teeth.

This model triceratops was created from scientific facts and some imagination.

The artists at one museum wanted to build an apatosaurus, a giant plant-eating dinosaur. They made a "skeleton" of plywood, and this framework was covered with wire screen. The screen was carefully bent to form the size and shape of the apatosaurus's body. The "skin" was made of layers of brown paper towels that had been dipped in white glue. After the paper towels were dry, the artists painted the huge creature with brown tile cement. The artists studied the dinosaur and decided its skin was too smooth and shiny for a *real* dinosaur. So one artist used a blowtorch to heat up the tile cement just enough to make it bubble and crack. The apatosaurus's skin was finished.

The wooden apatosaurus's neck is shaped with a wire screen.

Paper towels soaked in glue
cover the wire-screen neck.

When the prehistoric swamp exhibit is completed, the apatosaurus will look
down on visitors at Fernbank Science Center in Atlanta.

9.
Dioramas: Natural Settings for Museum Wildlife

When the museum artists completed the taxidermy work on a colorful wild turkey, this beautiful bird was placed in a woodland diorama. A diorama is an exhibit of wildlife, plants, rocks, and other natural scenery.

Natural scenery is put into place.

The North Georgia mountains make a beautiful background for this diorama.

To prepare the woodland scene, a large background painting was done. It showed mountains and trees as well as sky and clouds. In front of this scene, artificial leaves were attached to real branches. The leaves were made by heat-pressing shapes into thin sheets of plastic.

An artist cut the shapes out and fastened them to wire stems. One branch needed 62 leaves!

Rocks for the exhibit were carved from foam and painted to look real.

Yellow poplar leaf shapes are cut out and fastened to wire stems.

Rocks of all sizes are carved out of foam.

This exhibit rock weighs only five pounds.

The finished exhibit shows the wild turkey in its natural woodland habitat.

The completed exhibit brought a small part of the woodlands inside for visitors to see.

Nature dioramas display natural happenings that people rarely see. Chipmunks at home beneath the ground, for example, are exhibited by using real taxidermy specimens of chipmunks and artificial soil.

The nest and tunnels of the chipmunk's burrow are exhibited for visitors.

How would an artist display an underwater scene? It is easy. Instead of water, the artist uses a sheet of hard plastic that looks like the surface of water. A special clear liquid that dries with a shiny, wet look is poured over the plastic. Insects, artificial plants, and animal models that are placed below this layer look as though they are underwater.

Water ripples form as the special liquid poured over the plastic hardens.

Insects are placed above and below the artificial water surface.

The habitat diorama is one fascinating way for museums to display wildlife and for visitors to learn about nature. The artists work hard to make all the wildlife in exhibits look alive. They know they have succeeded when they hear visitors ask, "Are those animals *real*?"

This white-tailed deer looks at home in its natural setting.

Glossary

artificial: Not natural; something manmade.

diorama: An exhibit that shows plants and animals in their natural homes. It is also called a habitat display.

endangered species: A species that is threatened with extinction for some reason, such as over-hunting or loss of its habitat.

exhibit: A museum display.

fiberglass: A clothlike material made of tiny glass fibers. When combined with a special liquid, it dries hard to form a lightweight and sturdy material.

herpetologist: A person who studies reptiles.

Lepidoptera: An order of insects that includes moths and butterflies.

mold: An impression in plaster or other material. Molds are used to make replicas.

mount: To place the skin of a real animal onto an artificial body form.

papier-mâché: Lightweight material made of wet paper and glue.

plaster: A powder that is used to make molds. After it is mixed with water until creamy, it quickly sets up and dries hard.

prehistoric: Millions of years ago, before written history.

preservatives: Chemicals used to make something last a very long time.

replica: A copy or model of a real thing.

specimen: An animal used for study.

tan: To treat the skin of an animal with certain chemicals. A tanned skin will last a long time and stay soft.

taxidermy: The art of mounting the skins of animals onto artificial body forms.

Index

praying mantis, 47–52, **47, 48**
preservative
  injection of, 39, **39,** 45, **45**
  uses of, 3, 13, 16, 17, 22,
    23, 39, **39, 45**

replica
  bones, 57–58, **57, 59**
  See also models
reptiles
  making molds of, 24–25, **25,**
    28
  timber rattlesnake, 22–27,
    24, 25
  See also models, snake
rocks, artificial, 64, **65**

skeleton
  See dinosaurs
skins
  artificial, 58, 60, **61**
  preserving, 3, 5, **6,** 13
  removing, 2, 10, 13
soil, artificial, 67, **67**
spider
  See tarantula

tarantula, **42**
  freeze-drying of, 42–45, **44**
  displaying in clear plastic,
    45–46, **45, 46**

taxidermy, 7, 10, 13, 17, 62,
    67
  See also mounts, preparation
    of
timber rattlesnake, 22–27, **24,**
    25

water, artificial, **xvii,** 68, **68,**
    69
whistling swan, 12–15, **14, 15**
wildlife exhibit, xiii–xviii
  See also specific animals

ABOUT THE AUTHORS

Judy Cutchins grew up in Atlanta, Georgia. She has been teaching science and writing for children since 1974. Her Educational Specialist degree at Emory University concentrated on environmental science in the elementary schools. At Fernbank Science Center where she works with her co-author, Ginny Johnston, Ms. Cutchins produces quarterly science newsletters for school children, media sets and scripts for teachers, and science classroom presentations for grades K-7. Ms. Cutchins' love for "working vacations" has taken her recently on an Earthwatch expedition to Bermuda and to a sea mammal study program in New Hampshire where she accumulated a store of information for children's programs and newsletters.

Ginny Johnston has been a resident of Atlanta since 1964. Attending Emory and Georgia State Universities, she received B.A., M.Ed., and Educational Specialist degrees in elementary education. Since 1970 she has been an instructor of life sciences at Fernbank Science Center, developing and presenting programs for elementary students. Mrs. Johnston co-authors a scientific newsletter that is distributed quarterly to all the elementary students in DeKalb County, Georgia. In addition to teaching, she enjoys participating in scientific expeditions and field studies.

Ginny and her husband, Rob, are great sports enthusiasts and enjoy traveling, boating, and tennis.